Animal Pranksters

Alligator Snapping Turtles

by Julie Murray

2

Dash!
LEVELED READERS
An Imprint of Abdo Zoom • abdobooks.

2 Dash!
LEVELED READERS

Level 1 – Beginning
Short and simple sentences with familiar words or patterns for children who are beginning to understand how letters and sounds go together.

Level 2 – Emerging
Longer words and sentences with more complex language patterns for readers who are practicing common words and letter sounds.

Level 3 – Transitional
More developed language and vocabulary for readers who are becoming more independent.

THIS BOOK CONTAINS
RECYCLED MATERIALS

abdobooks.com

Published by Abdo Zoom, a division of ABDO, PO Box 398166, Minneapolis, Minnesota 55439. Copyright © 2023 by Abdo Consulting Group, Inc. International copyrights reserved in all countries. No part of this book may be reproduced in any form without written permission from the publisher. Dash!™ is a trademark and logo of Abdo Zoom.

Printed in the United States of America, North Mankato, Minnesota.
052022
092022

Photo Credits: Animals Animals, Getty Images, Minden Pictures, Science Source, Shutterstock
Production Contributors: Kenny Abdo, Jennie Forsberg, Grace Hansen, John Hansen
Design Contributors: Candice Keimig, Neil Klinepier

Library of Congress Control Number: 2021950314

Publisher's Cataloging in Publication Data

Names: Murray, Julie, author.
Title: Alligator snapping turtles / by Julie Murray.
Description: Minneapolis, Minnesota : Abdo Zoom, 2023 | Series: Animal pranksters | Includes online resources and index.
Identifiers: ISBN 9781098228323 (lib. bdg.) | ISBN 9781644947593 (pbk.) | ISBN 9781098229160 (ebook) | ISBN 9781098229580 (Read-to-Me ebook)
Subjects: LCSH: Alligator snapping turtle--Juvenile literature. | Turtles--Juvenile literature. | Reptiles--Behavior--Juvenile literature. | Zoology--Juvenile literature.
Classification: DDC 597.92--dc23

Table of Contents

Alligator Snapping Turtles

Alligator snapping turtles are only found in the United States.

They are freshwater turtles. They live in rivers, lakes, and swamps.

They are big turtles! Males are about 26 inches (66 cm) long. They weigh about 175 pounds (79 kg). Females are smaller.

They have large heads with beak-like jaws. They have big, sharp claws.

Alligator snapping turtles can be black, brown, or greenish in color. Their shells are often covered in **algae**.

They get their name from their shell. The shell's spiked ridges look like alligator skin.

Trick of the Tongue

An alligator snapping turtle has a long, pinkish tongue. It looks like a worm. It is used to "prank" **prey**.

The turtle lies still. It moves its tongue back and forth. This lures the **prey** toward the turtle's mouth.

Then the turtle grabs its **prey** with its strong jaws! Alligator snapping turtles hunt fish, frogs, and snakes.

More Facts

- Alligator snapping turtles are the largest freshwater turtles in the United States.

- They are an ancient **species**. They have been around for 20 to 90 million years!

- They can stay underwater for 50 minutes at a time.

Glossary

algae – organisms that live mainly in water and make their food through photosynthesis. Algae are different from plants in that they have no true leaves, roots, or stems.

prey – an animal that is hunted by other animals for food.

species – a group of living things that can have young with one another but not with those of other groups.

Index

claws 11

color 12

food 16, 19, 21

habitat 5, 6

head 11

hunting 16, 19, 21

jaws 11, 21

shell 12, 14

size 9

tongue 16

United States 5

weight 9

Online Resources

Booklinks
NONFICTION NETWORK
FREE! ONLINE NONFICTION RESOURCES

To learn more about alligator snapping turtles, please visit **abdobooklinks.com** or scan this QR code. These links are routinely monitored and updated to provide the most current information available.